Smoke & Mirrors

Smoke & Mirrors

Michael Faudet

Andrews McMeel
PUBLISHING®

For Lang,

You are the wish that came true.

Smoke & Mirrors

INTRODUCTION

Words are strange creatures.

They have a delightful habit of sneaking up on you when you least expect it. Where they come from is still a mystery to me. Maybe the heart, perhaps our imagination, quite possibly another dimension we are yet to discover.

I do know, however, where my words eventually end up.

Smoke & Mirrors is my third book and another precarious journey into that fragile world where love and loss share the same unmade bed.

All revealed within a collection of poetry, prose, and short stories.

Sometimes bittersweet.

Other times, walking that delicate fine line between dirty and delightfully pretty.

So welcome to *Smoke & Mirrors*.

Where the unexpected is to be expected.

I hope you enjoy reading this book as much as I did writing it for you.

All my love,

—Michael xo

BELIEVE

"I believe in you." Words that water flowers.

Anticipation

Anticipation
   is the breath we take,
   a silent pause
   with lips awake,
   a lingering kiss
   two lovers make,
   to be with you
   I cannot wait,
   each passing day
   I contemplate—

Anticipation
   is the breath we take.

DESTINED TO BE YOURS

It is in the quietest of moments,
    the silent pause found
    in twilight hue,
    when the sun
    slips behind the horizon,
    lost to a single
    purple pen stroke—
    I find myself
    thinking of you.

How your eyes
    reflect the moon
    in mine,
    reminding me
    of a love
    greater than
    the universe—
    our destiny written
    in the stars.

LISTEN TO YOUR HEART

Nobody knows your heart better than you. Trust your instincts. Never let anyone cast a shadow over your sunshine.

JUST HOLD ME TIGHT

You can't remove my scars or rewrite the past that haunts me.
Just hold me tight and tell me everything's going to be okay.

BETRAYAL

You held my heart in hands cupped—
a chalice emptied
by love's betrayal,
treachery concealed
within a kiss,
the poison sipped
by innocent lips.

SWEPT AWAY

You were the sea
    that swept me away,
    only to leave
    me adrift—
    far from the shore,
    my legs
    growing tired,
    of the lies
    that you said,
    out of my depth—
    in deep water
    I tread.

I Wish

I wish I could apologize for falling in love with you but I can't.
It would be like asking me to be sorry for breathing.

A Beautiful Deception

It was such a beautiful deception.

Like watching a summer storm light up the night sky without a single note of thunder heard.

Kissing your lips.

Drunk on the sweet nectar of corruption.

Never thinking my trust would be betrayed with a backward glance and smiling eyes.

As you closed the front door.

—

A single ping.

The text that wasn't meant for me arrived.

A sip of rancid milk.

The ugly perfume of decaying roses.

A wasp stinging a bee.

———

"If you could go back in time and give yourself some advice, what would it be?"

"Even the most eloquent lie becomes vulgar when exposed to the truth."

LOVE

Love is the double-edged sword that conquers hearts but can also cut the hand that wields it.

FREEDOM

It was another night lost in paradise.

Swaying palm trees caressed by a warm tropical breeze blowing gently from a moonlit sea.

She lit the cigarette he had made her give up. Her quiet act of defiance a release from a habit far worse than the curling smoke inhaled with smiling lips.

Blond hair falling over sun-kissed shoulders.

The old bruises painted by his fingertips fading to a lighter shade of yellow in the flickering glow of a swinging kerosene lantern.

As she walked slowly away from the beach house that had become her private sanctuary.

Far from the broken shards of a heart swept under the rug by a lover incapable of love.

"Listen to me. I know what's best for you."

He never really knew her at all.

How she yearned for something more than the cage he had built with golden bars.

Keeping her trapped within the insecurities that he created.

Sabrina ripped the necklace from her delicate throat. The pearls spilling down the steps made of driftwood and dry seaweed, like all the empty promises he had made, falling from cruel lips.

Her freedom now found beneath the twinkling stars.

Standing naked on the wet sand, swirling salty water running between her toes.

Remembering the words her mother once said, all those years ago.

The wisdom finally understood.

—

"Run toward your dream and never let anyone fill your pockets with rocks."

BLACK AND WHITE

It was a love that transcended even the most vibrant of colors, beautiful in its simplicity—written in black and white upon two beating hearts for all the world to read.

The Bedroom

It was the end
    of the beginning,
    beneath tangled sheets
    and sighing breath,
    sex blushing pink
    between your legs,
    open to the possibility
    of more to come,
    fingernails writing
    unfinished lines
    down my back,
    the scratches raw
    and incomplete,
    a river still running
    whispering my name,
    desire growing
    again and again—
    and again.

FAITH

Love is a little like religion. You need to have faith before miracles can happen.

A MORNING IN PARIS

She wore the perfume
  of pages turned,
  the scent of old books
  upon delicate fingers,
  a hint of sunshine
  captured within curls
  of windswept hair.

A morning made
  with poetry
  and swirling milk,
  in coffee sipped
  while Paris wakes,
  the words she read
  in dawn's pale light—
  how butter melts
  on warm croissants.

A Muse

She was a muse
    cursed with melancholia,
    her tears the ink
    on my typewriter ribbon.

LAST SUMMER

Her skin was the color of burnt caramel, so beautiful and almost glowing in the dying rays of a sleepy sun. Brown eyes melting, sweet and sugary, like the marshmallows we threaded onto crooked twigs and held over a flickering campfire.

How could I possibly resist those lips which searched for mine? As the night descended to the sound of squeaking bats flying overhead, their flapping wings skimming the treetops.

You pressed your back against the moss-covered wooden planks of a decaying boat shed. A shimmering moon swimming in the still waters of the rippling lake. Your hand reaching down, hitching up your skirt. My hand pulling your panties to one side.

We fucked.

Your legs wrapped around my waist, hips pushing hard into me, mouth slowly opening, a lock of black curly hair falling across your flushed cheeks.

—

We sat on the grassy bank, reeds swaying in rhythm to the chorus of early morning birdsong.

Your head resting on my shoulder, my finger tracing the contour of your neck.

If only time could stop and this happiness last forever.

—

"When I'm with you, love needs no explanation. It just is and we just are."

Lonely

So magnificent
    this mask I wear,
    my smile drawn
    with a broken
    yellow crayon,
    the loneliness
    concealed,
    in a garden
    of plastic flowers—
    my life revealed.

FAME

We drank martinis
    with cigarettes lit,
    the hedonist dream
    in limousines driven,
    the love we took
    no quarter given,
    our empty eyes—
    behind sunglasses
    hidden.

MY FLOWER

You were impossible to resist. I was like a bee seduced by a flower on a glorious spring day.

PATHWAYS

There were so many paths I could have taken in my life. Like the one that ran by the riverbank, where wild roses grew with sharp thorns. Or perhaps I should have followed my instincts and explored the track that wound its way through a dark and mysterious forest.

However, I ended up choosing the path of least resistance. The one that looked the easiest. Only to discover it was made of quicksand.

Hide-and-Seek

There were days when it seemed like I was trapped in an endless game of hide-and-seek with myself.

TRUE LOVE WAITS

She was my spring, a rosebud opening in the watery sunshine. This whimsical girl with grass-stained knees, her panties crumpled around a pale ankle.

A gorgeous lie kept secret from the world.

Far away from the prying eyes of a clueless boyfriend.

A delicious affair hidden within the twisted trees and rolling green hills. A story of two women madly in love, biding their time, before running away barefoot, to be lost forever.

———

"Do you ever feel guilty?" she asked, clutching a flower to her chest.

"Yes," I replied. "But only because it has taken me so long to realize who I am and what truly stirs my heart."

ALL OF ME

You wanted all of me but I had nothing more to give.

PRETTY WRISTS

Pretty wrists
    tied and tethered,
    a blindfold worn—
    black stockings
    and leather,
    pink stripper heels
    bound together,
    the freedom
    she feels,
    unchained
    forever.

THE KITTY CLUB

I'm not sure whose idea it was but it all seemed to make sense at the bottom of a vodka bottle.

Sophia tripping over the cat, correcting herself with her bare arms outstretched, walking over to the fridge on tiptoes. A tipsy girl in floral panties, smudged red lipstick, and messy hair.

All I can remember, through the haze of slurred words and the chinking of shot glasses, was that the sex had been amazing.

"You're out of milk," she shouted. Hanging off the fridge door like a sheet that had lost one peg on a clothesline.

"There's some ice cream in the freezer. Maybe you can use that. I'm okay with black anyway, the stronger the coffee, the better."

Well, I think that's how the conversation went.

—

The new morning streamed through my bedroom window, waking me in the worst possible way.

A dazzling beam of bright sunlight blinding my squinting eyes and my head pounding.

I sat up out of bed, hovered for a matter of seconds, before collapsing back onto the pillows.

Sophia danced into the bedroom, headphones on, and threw a bottle of water onto the bed. She flashed me a smile, did a little shimmy, and danced out of the room.

She was wearing one of my shirts and nothing else.

I felt a familiar stirring under the sheet.

A hangover hard-on.

I reached for the bottle of water and cursed my stupidity for falling into the vodka trap. By now I should have known better than to try to keep up with her. I always paid a shocking price.

"You should think about hopping into the shower."

Sophia's shouted command from the lounge made me wince as a foggy memory descended over my fuzzy brain.

I closed my eyes and visualized the promise I had made the night before.

Now I remembered.

It had been my idea to take Sophia to the Kitty Club for lunch.

What the hell had I been thinking?

—

The codeine had finally kicked in and I started to feel human again.

Sitting in the white leather back seat of Sophia's silver Bentley, driven by her pretty assistant, Marie.

My head propped up against the window watching the trees whizz by.

Sophia had arranged the ride while I was drowning in the shower, the cold water slapping my body back to life.

Marie had also brought over a change of clothes for her.

"What do you think? Skirt short enough?"

I turned and gazed at Sophia's outfit.

The gray woolen pleated skirt riding up, giving a flash of red satin panties, her long black-stockinged legs attached to a pair of pale pink stripper heels.

Her look neatly finished off with a tight, body-hugging, buttoned white blouse.

"I think if you're going for kinky secretary chic, you've excelled yourself."

"Funny man. Let's see who has the last laugh when we get to the club."

I'd almost forgotten about why we were hurtling along the back-country road.

My dumb idea.

I had never been to the Kitty Club but heard they served up a fabulous seafood lunch and swinging sex as dessert.

There had been a write-up about the place in *Outrageous* magazine, and Sophia was all in when I casually mentioned it to her in between shots of vodka.

Marie hit the horn.

A group of ducks flew up from the road, narrowly missing the windscreen.

She then spun the wheel, doing a hand brake turn, sliding the Bentley into a tight left-hand corner.

"Fuck! What the fuck!" I yelled, my head slamming back into the headrest.

Sophia grinned and patted my leg.

"Look, we're almost there," said Marie laughing.

The Bentley slowed down to an elegant purr as it rolled up the gravel driveway, a row of conifer trees lining the sides.

I could see a sandstone manor perched on a hill in the near distance.

"It looks so gorgeous," Sophia sighed.

———

We were met at the steps by two gentlemen dressed in identical white tuxedos and dark sunglasses.

One of them took the keys from Marie and the other handed us each a narrow black velvet mask.

"Discretion is everything," he said politely as the three of us put on the masks.

We looked like well-dressed cat burglars.

"Now just take the steps up to the main door and please wait to be seated."

Sophia took a £50 note from her Prada handbag and tried to give the tip to the attendant.

He waved his hand and smiled.

"No need," he said. "It's our pleasure to have you as our guests."

We walked up the steps and pushed open the heavy wooden door which led to a grand marble hallway and antique reception desk. Where we were greeted by a well-dressed elderly woman, who looked like she had stepped out of a classic, black and white, 1940s Hollywood movie.

"Welcome to the Kitty Club!" she said warmly. "Now before I take you to your table, I just want to tell you about the house rules. First, treat everyone with respect and remember no means no. Secondly, the club has the right to remove any guest who is rude or gets drunk. The third rule is terribly important; all gentlemen must wear a condom when performing. Lastly, have fun, my dears!"

Sophia leaned over and whispered into my ear.

"I hope you paid close attention to the second rule."

"My name is Edna, and if you need anything or have any questions, please just ask one of our waiters. If you'd be so very kind to settle your account now, it makes everything so much easier."

Sophia handed over her black Amex card to Edna, who swiped it and handed it back along with a small green velvet bag.

"Just a few things you might need for later," she said with a cheeky smile.

———

We were seated in the grand dining room by our waitress, Penelope, a stunning blonde dressed in a neatly pressed French maid's outfit.

The table was covered by a pristine white tablecloth, with silver cutlery and white bone china plates sitting perfectly upon it.

A vase of red roses placed in the middle.

I sat down and scanned the room, trying not to look too obvious.

The other guests all wore the same masks and were immaculately dressed. Deep in conversation and it seemed like a mixture of ages.

Penelope handed us each a brown leather-bound menu with the words "Kitty Club" embossed on the front.

"As you can see, today we are serving our famous seafood selection platter, with a choice of three vintage champagnes. If you are a vegan, our chef is also serving a gorgeous wild mushroom lasagna with shaved white truffles and garden-picked asparagus, lemon-infused olive oil, and roasted almonds."

Marie's face lit up and she could hardly contain her smile.

"Well, that's me decided. I'll definitely be having the lasagna."

Sophia looked over at me.

"Guess we'll be sharing the platter, then. What do you fancy for the selection?"

I scanned the menu.

There was a long list of delicious seafood to choose from and I could already feel my mouth salivating at the prospect of sampling the cuisine.

"I think the orange butter grilled lobsters are a must, two dozen of the natural oysters, sea urchin, the chili soft shell crab, and the vodka salmon gravlax sounds good too."

Penelope scribbled on her notepad with a pencil.

"And a side serve of the black caviar and parmesan hand-cut fries would be great," added Sophia.

"Excellent!" replied Penelope. "May I also suggest a bottle of the Krug '89 to get you started?"

"Wonderful! I can't wait." Sophia gave Penelope a sly wink.

Our waitress slid away and Marie opened the bag Edna had given us.

She comically held her hands to her mouth in shock.

Inside were a couple of tubes of lube and several condom packets.

I laughed.

Sophia giggled.

It was going to be an interesting lunch.

———

The food was magnificent.

After finishing off our second bottle of champagne we were led away from our table by Penelope, up a spiral staircase to "our bedroom." Most of the other guests had already left the dining room.

"You'll find some toiletries, toothbrushes, and toothpaste in the bathroom. Please take a shower and when you're done, enter the gold doorway at the end of the hall. You can hang your clothes in the wardrobe and there is a safe for your valuables too. Not that we have ever had anything stolen. You'll find dressing gowns in the wardrobe, all sizes, no need to wear anything underneath, and don't forget to take your green bag with you. Do you have any questions?"

Sophia smiled and lightly tapped Penelope's shoulder with her hand.

"Any chance you'll be joining the party later?"

Penelope grinned. "You just never know."

Our waitress walked out of the bedroom and closed the door with a quiet click.

"Oh my, check this out," called Marie from the bathroom.

Sophia and I entered the palatial en suite bathroom. It became instantly obvious what had caught Marie's attention. The shower cubicle was huge, with multiple showerheads.

"Room for all of us," Sophia chuckled.

"Why don't you girls go first? I'm going to take a look at those robes."

"You're such a bloody prude, seriously! Where is your sense of adventure? Look, Marie is game."

I ignored Sophia's teasing jibe and tried not to look at Marie as she unzipped the black dress she was wearing, letting it fall to the red and black tiled floor. Closely followed by a matching black bra and panties.

"I thought you were leaving, you pervert," laughed Sophia.

I left the two girls to it and returned to the bedroom. Opening the wardrobe I saw the collection of robes hanging inside. They were all made of red silk and I took one off the coat hanger.

I laid the robe onto the king-size bed and noticed a minibar tucked neatly away in the corner.

Opening the minibar fridge I found it stocked with rows and rows of little bottles of spirits. I reached in and took a bottle of Grey Goose vodka, unscrewed the cap, and swallowed the contents in one gulp.

It was then that I heard the loud moaning coming from the bathroom. Not even the hiss of the showerheads could disguise it.

Little did I know then, this would be nothing compared to what would happen next.

—

The gold door at the end of the hallway opened onto what could best be described as a ballroom. Except nobody was dancing beneath the dimly lit chandeliers.

Wherever I looked, couples and groups of masked naked bodies were engaged in all manner of sexual acts. On tables, leather couches, against the walls, and even on the emerald green carpet that covered the entire floor.

A young man with a massive erection walked over to us. He was wearing a white-colored mask.

"Welcome to the orgy room. My name is Jackson and I'm one of the hosts. I can take your robes."

Sophia whispered in my ear.

"Feeling a bit inadequate, are we?"

I gently pushed her away and removed my robe and handed it to Jackson.

"There you go," I said in my most cavalier voice.

My frequent visits to the beaches in the South of France had prepared me well for public nudity.

Marie and Sophia handed over their robes next.

"Now how many of these do you think you'll need?" said Marie, taking three condom packets from the bag we had been given and holding them up in her petite hand.

I took one.

Jackson laughed. "Oh, I think you'll be needing more than that."

Sophia reached over and started rubbing my flaccid cock.

I felt my cheeks flush red with embarrassment.

Which given the activity in the room did make me feel a little prudish.

It was like Jackson could read my mind and he quickly tried to put it at rest.

"Everyone has the first-time jitters, but believe me, just relax and go with it."

Marie must have already taken his advice to heart.

She dropped to her knees and performed her infamous party trick. Sliding a condom onto Jackson's hard cock with her mouth. He let out a deep groan as her pretty red lips covered the tip of his huge shaft.

I must admit her spontaneous act made my cock swell and stand to attention.

"Come on, let's go fuck," cooed Sophia, taking me by the hand and leading me over to a corner of the giant room.

I sat down on a large brown leather studded chair and slid on a condom. Sophia straddled me, guiding my hard cock into her tight wet pussy.

We started to fuck and it felt amazing. Maybe it was the sight of all the others doing it and the sounds of the orgy echoing throughout the ballroom that made the sex feel so hot.

A girl with blond hair leaned in between us. Despite her wearing a white mask I could tell it was our waitress from the dining room. She locked lips with Sophia, who reached down between Penelope's long legs and started rubbing her shaved pussy.

This just turned me on even more and I gripped Sophia's slender waist and fucked her harder, faster, and deeper.

When the orgasm hit, it did so with an intensity that made my whole body shudder.

Sophia hopped off me and laid down on the carpet, legs spread, while Penelope gently sucked on her swollen pink clitoris.

Jackson was right.

I certainly would need more than one condom to survive this debauched afternoon gathering.

—

The drive home was a sedate one.

We were so exhausted we hardly even noticed how beautiful the sunset was outside the windows of the Bentley.

Sophia was the first to break the silence. "Well, that was fun."

Always the champion of the understatement.

We all burst out laughing.

Marie looked into the rearview mirror.

"I thought the lasagna was one of the best things I've ever eaten."

"Second only to Jackson's cock," Sophia replied grinning.

"Well, I'm pleased you both enjoyed your lunch at the Kitty Club, one of my better ideas, I think," I said smugly.

Sophia pinched my arm with a mock expression of surprise on her beautiful face.

"Your idea? I distinctly remember it was me who suggested we go last night. Honestly, after a few vodkas you'd forget your head was attached to your neck."

I knew better than to get into a debate with Sophia.

—

A full moon was peeking slowly above the crooked rooftops of the tired terrace houses.

Loved-up couples, walking hand in hand, weaved their way along the narrow streets of Soho, stepping around the groups of drunk revelers looking for their next drink.

Marie pulled the Bentley up outside the glass doors of the Purple Palace, a small boutique hotel where Sophia stayed whenever she was in London.

"Would you like to come inside for a quick martini?"

Sophia saw the hesitation in my eyes. There was never such a thing as a quick martini or anything when it came to this girl.

"Or I can get Marie to run you back home?" she quickly added with a flutter of her gorgeous eyelashes.

She was the abridged version of all the love letters I had ever written. Beautifully concise and impossible to resist.

It was going to be another long night.

WHY CLOUDS CRY

When you walked out of my life, it was like the sun had completely vanished from the sky. I now know why clouds cry.

One Kiss

All it took was one kiss.

The tide running backward away from
    the beach.

Our love—

An unstoppable force building on
    the horizon.

Two hearts stranded on the shore.

Waiting for the tsunami to hit.

Lost Time

We always lived for tomorrow. Never for today. Now all that's left of our love is an unfinished yesterday.

CASABLANCA

Do you remember the night we watched *Casablanca* in bed, drinking sweet plum wine in teacups?

The light flickering across your rosy cheeks, black fringe framing your tipsy eyes. My hand beneath the sheets, a finger writing your initials on the inside of your thigh.

How we made love before the end credits rolled across the screen?

You kneeling, head pressed down into the pillow, while I fucked you from behind.

The mini earthquake between your legs as the orgasm came.

Have you forgotten how we ran upstairs like two naughty children, raiding the fridge for midnight snacks? A feast of hummus, tabouli, and toasted flatbread eaten by candlelight.

How we whispered *"I love you"* with our arms wrapped tightly around each other?

—

"Of course I remember. How could I possibly forget a memory tattooed onto my heart?"

Passing Seconds

How I love the slow seduction of the now. The moment when even passing seconds take a deep breath and all that matters is your eyes staring into mine.

A LONG-DISTANCE RELATIONSHIP

You texted me again.

A series of love heart emojis wrapped around a lengthy paragraph of typed words that said how much you were missing me.

My sun rising while yours was setting. A slow conversation between two lovers separated by time zones and circumstance.

We both knew it would be difficult living apart, but I had no idea just how empty our lives would become. Going to bed each night and waking up to nothing. Just a silent void. Broken by the chatter of a television switched on to give the illusion of company.

A cup of morning coffee made for one.

I still remember the day you burst through the front door, your voice giddy with excitement telling me the news that you had gotten the job. The moment when my heart sunk, hidden by a beaming smile and an enthusiastic hug.

"I'm just so happy for you!" I lied.

We drank the bottle of champagne that had been waiting in the fridge, *just in case*. Each mouthful a bitter reminder that I was actually going to lose you. Not that I let you know how I really felt. How could I? It was an opportunity of a lifetime, a dream come true for you.

Later that night we made love.

Afterward, as we lay in bed staring at the ceiling, you noticed something was wrong. Somehow you had seen beneath the veneer of happiness I had tried so desperately to project.

"It's only going to be for a year and then I'll be back. The time will fly by and we can spend all the holidays together," you whispered. Wrapping your arms around me. Trying to reassure me that everything was going to be alright.

I suddenly felt so incredibly guilty. Annoyed at my own selfishness. Of course we could make it work. We wouldn't be the first couple to have a long-distance relationship.

Kathy took my hand, her soft brown eyes staring into mine.

"I love you," she said reassuringly. "And nothing is ever going to change that."

———

One year has now turned into two years.

Our texts have got shorter. The Skype calls, less frequent.

"I don't want you to have to stay up so late during the week and anyway we can chat on the weekends, right?" she said.

You were always the logical one.

We both decided to skip the next holiday break too.

"Better we save the airfare money for a real holiday one day, to somewhere exotic. Maybe Tahiti," I said.

I can hear the birdsong outside the window while I make a morning coffee.

The sun streaming into the kitchen.

It's going to be a beautiful day.

—

Absence doesn't always make the heart grow fonder. Sometimes it just teaches us that we can live apart.

IT WAS OVER

A secret shared
    by quivering lips,
    the words escape
    in shades of blue,
    no eyes can hide
    in downward glance—
    a passing cloud
    across the sun.

A glass of red
    remains untouched,
    a quiet sigh
    is barely heard,
    the whisper
    of a summer breeze—
    lost within a chorus
    of singing cicadas.

When left unsaid
    so much is said,
    your silence—
    I understood.

DAMAGED GOODS

Do we not enter this world a little broken? Damaged goods
with awkward smiles. Searching for the glue we call love.

CARELESS WORDS

It was your careless words,
    laced with malice
    that drew blood
    upon wrists—
    that longed
    only to be kissed.

THE PARTY

My heart started to race the minute you entered the party, walking across the room toward me, a smile flashed in my direction.

There was something quite magical and weirdly hypnotic about you.

You wrapped one arm around my neck, kissed me quickly on the cheek, and playfully stroked my chin with your other hand.

"How are you?"

My eyes averted yours. In case the pretense of being *just friends* was revealed, the longing to be more, given away.

"All good, couldn't be better," I replied, slowly taking a step backward.

You gently ran a finger down my cheek, and before I could say anything more, you were gone.

I watched you walk away and vanish into the crowd of writhing bodies on the dance floor.

A pang of regret pounding deep inside my chest.

I knew our time had come and gone.

Yet here I was thinking about you again, retracing the steps of a relationship that was always destined to fail.

"I think it's best if we put all of this behind us and move on."

You were right, of course. No matter how hard I tried, you just weren't that into me. Not in the way I hoped for, dreamed about, and wished for night, after night, after night.

I remember I once read a short story about a girl who never left home. Preferring to live instead in a fantasy world of her own making rather than face the reality of life outside.

At the time it had seemed a ridiculous premise, and I felt a little frustrated by her lack of courage to open the front door and confront whatever the truth may be.

How quickly perceptions can change when love slams the door shut. Wiping the smile from your face in an instant. The shock of rejection, like a dagger plunged into your chest and twisted.

They say time heals all wounds.

I say, whoever said that doesn't have a fucking clue about how I felt about you.

Still feel about you.

NORWEGIAN WOOD

How I loved those summer evenings counting the stars while you read *Norwegian Wood* aloud to me——the sentences punctuated with warm kisses and sips of vodka.

She Ran

She ran,
    a trail of stardust in her wake,
    past a rising moon
    and fallen sun,
    across a sky
    of billowing black,
    running forward
    but returning back,
    to the place
    where dreams began,
    on pillows pink—
    the velvet crushed,
    an opium pipe
    in fingers held,
    two lovers kiss
    with smoky lips,
    a trace of lemon
    and honey spilt,
    her sleepy eyes
    a patchwork quilt,
    all magic sewn
    with golden needle,
    upon an arm
    with purple thread,
    a pencil writes
    another sentence,
    a circle drawn

where it began,
another dream,
a new beginning,
across a sea
of poppies red—
she runs.

One More Touch

I love how your hips rise, reaching the point of no return,
fingers gripping the sheets—my hand between your legs.

IN YOUR ARMS

Billowing clouds painted lilac,
    splashes of pale pink
    across a dawning sky,
    your smile illuminated
    by glowing shafts
    of morning sunlight,
    the sound of crashing waves
    on a beach below,
    another day
    in your arms—
    begun.

Chance Meeting

I still remember how we first met.

A late-night conversation on a plane, nervous words exchanged between the turbulence, your hand reaching out for mine when the shaking got worse.

Two strangers seeking solace from the storm.

A chance meeting, totally random, the odds firmly fixed against us, yet somehow love found a way to beat them.

By the time we had landed, phone numbers were exchanged, and a promise to do lunch sometime was made with the un-clicking of a seat belt.

—

How quickly the years have passed.

The lemon tree we planted, the one you bought us as a housewarming gift, all grown up and bearing fruit.

Speckles of dying paint peeling on the cobwebbed veranda.

Two cats and a canary sleeping peacefully underground.

A shoebox kept under the stairs, filled with Valentine's Day cards and fading photographs.

Another bottle of wine empty.

—

Tonight we made love.

Rain lashing the bedroom windows, trees swaying, their creaking branches arm wrestling with a howling wind.

Flashes of lightning illuminating your face in the dark.

Reminding me of the young girl I fell in love with on some faraway plane.

How your hand reached out for mine.

And how love came and took hold of our hearts.

Never to let go again.

POETRY

The head can guide the hand that wields the pen but poetry can only be written by the heart.

THE HANGING TREE

There was no warning.

No note.

Nothing.

Yesterday we were just two old friends catching up, sitting cross-legged on a picnic blanket under a walnut tree. Sharing a bottle of Jack Daniels, reliving past memories in a beautiful garden on a balmy summer's afternoon.

"Do you remember the first time we kissed in high school?"

If only you knew how many times I've cried today, answering that very question, over and over again inside my head.

You seemed so happy.

So full of life.

Your wonderful blue eyes squinting in the orange haze of a setting sun.

I can still feel the warmth of your hand holding mine.

If only I had never let go.

The Love We Share

The love we share
    with open hearts,
    overflowing—
    like a river
    bursting its banks.

And when we fuck
    how beautiful
    the night—
    a firework show
    on the 4th of July.

A DANGEROUS SEA

Lust is a dangerous sea—
    the rocks concealed,
    a lighthouse dark,
    our hearts shipwrecked—
    by a crashing wave
    of complicity.

HER VOICE

Whenever you spoke, your voice was like music. A symphony composed by the very lips I longed to kiss.

THE HUNGER

You gave me that look—eyes wild, pupils dilated. Sitting on the edge of the kitchen bench. Your orange dress hitched up, a busy hand between your legs.

"Fuck me."

The intensity of your words piercing a cloud of thin smoke coming from the oven.

A lasagna burning.

Forgotten.

LETTING GO

A single raindrop
    clinging to a withered leaf,
    the last sip of vodka
    slowly slipping down
    a tilted glass,
    a cigarette dying
    by a riverbank,
    the last strand
    of winter hair
    turning gray,
    ink drying
    on a page,
    all memory
    of you,
    quietly fading
    away.

I DREAMT OF YOU

You opened my heart
    while I lay sleeping,
    fingers turning
    a broken lock,
    the combination
    I was keeping,
    you remembered
    while I forgot.

A second chance
    another meeting,
    a chasm breached
    with spoken words,
    forgiveness found
    not mine for keeping,
    in waking dream
    all hope is lost.

HOW CAN I MOVE ON?

How can I move on?
    When every single muscle
    inside this broken body
    refuses to wake,
    paralyzed by grief
    and desperation.

My trembling hands
    unable to grasp,
    the fragile pieces
    of love's jigsaw puzzle,
    scattered by a wind
    which changed
    without warning,
    a new direction
    decided by you,
    on a careless whim
    with no explanation.

Here, take my heart
with hammer held,
and finish the job
your words so
poorly started,
leave me empty
no trace of dust,
erase all memory
and delete the past,
squeeze the last
drop from my
crying eyes,
for until you do
how can I move on?

COLD COMFORT

You became invisible,
    a ghost haunting
    the ruins of a heart
    left broken,
    where love
    once burned,
    so quickly taken,
    like a bucket
    of water
    thrown on a fire,
    all trace
    of warmth—
    forsaken.

Rena

It was her eyes
    that sang the songs—
    with a voice
    that reminded me
    of rainy nights
    and opium.

Like a runaway kite
    lost to the wind,
    summer storms
    and circus swings.

And when she sings—
    a spell is cast,
    her rose petal lips
    breaking hearts.

NIA

Twenty candles
    burning bright.

A love composed
    its rhythm kept—
    by beating heart
    and bass guitar.

A violet held
    in summer's hand.

My birthday wish,
    your happiness.

Perspective

The further we run away from our heart, the quicker we lose sight of who we really are.

DEATH

It wasn't death that frightened me.

What really terrified me was not knowing when I would hold you in my arms again.

———

"We're soul mates," she whispered. "A love like ours can never be lost. Not now, not ever. When you take your last breath, it will just be a momentary pause in time, before our lips find each other once more."

Empty Space

I woke up,
    not with the gentle
    stirring of sheets
    against my skin,
    or your alarm—
    Amy Winehouse
    singing "Rehab"
    on an iPhone,
    but to an empty space—
    the one you
    left behind.

The Love You Give

It is your heart that beats within my body. The love you give—
the blood that runs through my veins.

A WINTER'S DAY

Her touch felt like a summer's day in the middle of winter.

Warm against my chilly skin, fingers stroking my neck as we sat at our favorite spot in the park, on an old moss-covered wooden bench that overlooked the duck pond and had a view of a church spire in the distance.

"What do you think is the secret to staying in love?" Lucy asked.

"Never giving up on each other," I replied, putting my arm around her shoulders.

She was wearing the orange puffer jacket I had bought her. Last year's birthday present that came with an airplane ticket hidden in the pocket. A surprise skiing trip to Aspen.

Lucy sighed. "Not always easy to do."

I smiled and thought about her words. She was right. I remembered all the times I had fought for love in the past, trying to save a relationship, only to lose the battle in the end.

"No, it's not easy to do. Sometimes hanging onto love is like rubbing two wet sticks together to make a fire with tired hands."

Lucy kissed me on the cheek and slid her hands under my coat, reaching down inside my jeans.

"Well, these hands are far from tired," she whispered.

—

"Do you still love me?"

"More than all the words I have ever written. More than all the words I will ever write."

A BEAUTIFUL CONUNDRUM

She was a mysterious girl, impossible to predict—a beautiful conundrum that kept me awake on stormy nights.

FAR AWAY

You have gone,
    somewhere far away
    beyond the reach
    of these hands,
    wishing for yours—
    the touch of skin
    against skin
    in a warm shower,
    a memory reset
    by the cycle
    of a smiling sun
    and crying moon,
    my lips quietly
    counting down
    the days,
    until your eyes
    hold mine again,
    and our love
    is the only thing
    we can see.

ROLLER COASTERS

All that we seek
    only confusion found,
    in vodka shots
    and empty pill bottles,
    writing love letters
    never sent,
    riding roller coasters
    on rusty rails—
    our lives spent,
    living the lie
    but holding
    onto the dream,
    the sweet scent
    of youth
    corrupted—
    by the reality
    of tomorrow.

BEFORE

In the dying darkness—
    before the dawn wakes
    from its slumber,
    and a tired moon
    falls gently
    back to sleep,
    before the first note
    by magpie sung,
    beneath the covers
    of a restless bed—
    the softest of moans
    breaking the silence,
    a sinking star
    in a sea of black,
    before a summer sun
    rises in the East,
    from open lips
    comes the scream
    of sweet release.

Run Away

All I ever wanted, the only wish I ever had, was to run away with you and never stop running.

Just Friends

It was her tightly held independence that stirred my heart the most.

How she lived life on her terms.

A runaway girl with stormy gray eyes staring out to the shimmering horizon.

Always the driver and never the passenger.

Slender hands gripping the leather-bound steering wheel of a purring silver convertible.

The midday sun beating down on a lonely desert road to nowhere.

A trace of perfume trailing in the wind from a neck I longed to caress. Her sideways glance in my direction, flashing me a rare smile with red lipsticked lips.

"Brand New Moves" by Hey Violet playing on the radio.

A lock of blond hair quickly swept away from her face.

Always in control.

Like the words she whispered to me last night in the tiny motel room.

"We fuck but we never kiss."

A line in the sand drawn with her finger across my bare chest.

One we never crossed.

Just friends.

SECOND BEST

The tragedy
    of the dispossessed,
    those lonely souls
    with love—
    obsessed,
    no tears
    can put a heart
    to rest,
    when chasing
    a dream—
    and settling
    for second best.

ALL THE THINGS

Just the very sound of your voice can bring me to my knees and make me think of all the things I'd love to do but dare not say.

SANDCASTLES

We built our sandcastles with hands entwined. The waves breaking between kisses melting upon lips sticky and sweet. The memory of pink cotton candy and strawberry ice cream mixed with a single sigh and a whispered "I love you."

A heart traced with a wet stick you found under the pier, our names left behind for the sea to steal with white frothy fingers.

I can still hear you singing.

A spiral shell pressed to my ear.

Your voice laced with salty wind and sailing ships.

A siren calling me.

My mind drifting back to our last summer.

—

I caught a glimpse of you, the fluttering of a floral dress and a billowing lock of red hair, fading into a crowd of coffee-drinking strangers.

Taking a seat somewhere at the back of the busy café.

A year had passed since we last spoke but time had done nothing to still my beating heart. A deep pang of uncertainty rising from the pit of my stomach.

I buried my head back into my newspaper, trying to hide and not be seen, while my mind desperately tried to make sense of the conflicting emotions racing through it.

"Leave now, slip away unnoticed, escape while you still can … talk to her."

The sweet scent of patchouli made the decision for me.

"Hi there, mind if I join you?"

I peered up from the pages, my eyes meeting the same gorgeous smile that haunted my memory during sleepless nights.

Daisy stood in front of me, her delicate hands pressed down on the edge of the table.

"Of course, please, sit down. How are you?"

My startled words betrayed the awkwardness I felt, a heady mixture of exhilaration and panic pulsing through my body.

"Oh, I'm fine," she replied, pulling out a chair and sitting down next to me. "A little jet-lagged, but nothing a shot of strong coffee and a glass of Pernod can't fix. I wasn't sure if it was you, but then I noticed the watch."

I smiled. It was always the little things, the tiny details that caught you out in the end. In this case, it was the Rolex with its distinctive blue face and matching blue leather strap on my right wrist that had given me away. A parting gift from her. The irony not lost on me.

"You look as beautiful as always. So, where did you fly in from?"

Before Daisy could answer, a waiter pushed in between us, pencil poised, ready to take an order.

"Can I get you something?" he inquired with a heavy French accent.

"Sure. Two short blacks, a Pernod on ice, make that two. Thank you."

The waiter scribbled down my order and left as abruptly as he came.

Daisy leaned in and spoke in a hushed voice. "Why do you always come here? The staff are so rude."

"Yes, they are, but the view makes up for it and I'm a creature of habit."

The Café de Mer lived up to its name. Perched high on a clifftop, overlooking the beach below and thunderous waves breaking onto the jagged rocks.

"So tell me, what made you come back here?" I asked.

I could see the subtle change in her expression, like a cloud passing quickly in front of the sun.

"I don't know. Maybe because I thought I might find you here." Her hand reached across the table and held mine. "I've missed you."

I pulled my hand away. The old bitterness returning, catching me unaware.

"Well, whose fault is that? You never even said goodbye. All I got was a crumpled note that explained nothing and this watch left on the pillow."

I stood up, the anger pulsing through my veins.

Daisy gave me a pleading look. "Please don't leave."

"Two short blacks and two Pernods."

The waiter placed the cups and glasses on the table.

I waited for him to go before giving my answer.

"Give me one good reason why I should stay."

A lone tear ran down her cheek, a trembling hand reaching for mine again. A sad smile returning to Daisy's lips.

"I'm dying."

———

I threw the shell away.

Sending it spinning into the sea.

Daisy's voice fading beneath the sparkling blue where her ashes lay scattered.

I now understood why she left me.

It was love that drove her away from my arms.

Her way of trying to shield me from the dreadful truth that would take her from me forever.

"I wanted you to remember the good times."

And it was love that made her return.

The distance between us more painful to bear than the hidden death that crept silently through her bones.

We spent the last few months as lovers often do.

Lost in our own world of make believe, hiding from reality, living each day as if it was our first.

Walking along the beach at sunset.

Hands entwined.

Building our sandcastles.

A Perfect Day

Dappled light
   plays hide-and-seek,
   with summer leaves
   of rustling green,
   the restless swans
   in rippling pond,
   your hand in mine
   where it belongs,
   a pale blue sky
   with red balloons,
   a coffee stirred
   with plastic spoon,
   a park-side view
   our kisses sent—
   from trembling lips
   and melting hearts,
   how lovers pass
   a perfect day.

THE CURSE

You were a curse
    gift-wrapped in poetry,
    breaking hearts
    with broken verse.

DEPRESSION

There were days when it seemed like the whole world was against me.

Hell-bent on destroying what little confidence I had left.

My hands desperately trying to grip onto the last strands of sanity—bare white knuckles clenched tight.

A big black dog I called *Depression* held my life in its powerful jaws.

Threatening my very existence with its razor-sharp fangs.

And just when I thought I would finally be totally consumed, my life ripped to shreds, somehow you were always there to rescue me.

To kiss away the unhappiness and self-doubt from my quivering lips.

Holding back the grim darkness with your reassuring words.

"Everything is going to be okay."

THE WORDS YOU SAY

Of all the things
    you've said to me,
    sometimes rainbows
    other times storms,
    it's the red roses
    you plant inside my heart,
    that I remember,
    every time you say
    the words—
    I love you.

STAY TOGETHER

Never say never
    nor question whether,
    two distant hearts
    can stay together,
    for true love
    is a ship,
    that can sail
    in any weather.

DREAMING

When you hold me in your arms, there are times when I have
to pinch myself. Just to remind me I'm not dreaming.

BLACK STOCKINGS

You were naked.

Except for a pair of sheer black stockings you wore with matching heels. Sitting on a hard wooden chair with your knees apart.

"I have a little surprise for you."

I watched as your fingers reached down and slowly tore a hole in the crotch of the stockings. Your eyes never leaving mine as more of your pussy was exposed with each rip of the fabric.

"Shame to ruin such a pretty pair of stockings," I replied.

Sophia laughed and opened her legs wider.

"Well, perhaps it's your turn to ruin me."

———

"Do you think I'm kinky?"

"No. I think you're a girl blessed with a vivid imagination."

THE WORDS YOU SPOKE

It was your words
    I missed the most,
    softly spoken
    in winter gray,
    beautiful—
    spilling from lips
    like falling snow
    in late November,
    every conversation
    a poem written,
    melting my heart—
    so warm,
    so wonderful,
    so unforgettable—
    the words
    you spoke.

CRY FOR ME

Cry for me,
    not when I'm dead,
    for that will be too late—
    cry for me now
    while I'm still here,
    to kiss your tears
    away.

THE MEANING OF LIFE

"What do you think the meaning of life is?" she asked, staring up at the stars.

I blew a spiraling plume of smoke from a glowing joint into the warm night air.

"To love and be loved," I replied.

"Oh, really? I always thought it was a large bowl of vanilla ice cream with strawberries on top."

YOU LIVED FOR BOOKS

You lived for books,
    lost within a dusty world
    of turned pages,
    each sentence read
    a breath drawn,
    every word—
    the blood
    rushing through
    your veins,
    how I wished
    I was a story,
    inside a book,
    held lovingly
    in your hands,
    never to be
    put down.

LOVE YOURSELF

Sometimes we are so generous with our love, so willing to give it all away, that we leave nothing behind for ourselves.

MY FAULT

My words—
    poorly chosen,
    ill spoken,
    screamed
    into a fierce wind,
    a mistake
    blown back,
    misdirected,
    now directed—
    at a heart,
    I alone
    have broken.

STAY STRONG

Even the darkest of days will pass. A cloud cannot hide the sun forever.

The Missing Sock

"I think I'm going mad," Lucy said with her head buried in a drawer, hands tossing different-colored socks onto the bedroom carpet.

Her sudden exclamation caught my attention, enough to tear me away from the book I was reading, *The Anthology of Wailing Ghosts* by Victor Varnish.

"There's no risk of that happening, you went mad years ago," I laughed.

Lucy turned and gave me *that stare*, the one that took a handful of confusion and threw it into a blender with a sprinkling of annoyance.

She held up one white knee-length sock and dangled it in front of me.

"Have you seen the other one? I can't find it anywhere."

I leaned forward in the bed, took a closer look, and shook my head.

"No, I haven't. Socks have a habit of going missing."

—

We lay in bed, the end credits from *The Shining* rolling up the television screen. It was one of our favorite movies and we never got tired of watching it.

I noticed the puzzled expression written across Lucy's brow as she reached for another pistachio nut from the bowl. Her nimble fingers quickly breaking the salty outer shell and popping the greenish-purple kernel into her mouth.

"What's wrong?" I asked.

Lucy started to chuckle, picking up another pistachio.

"It's that bloody sock! I can't stop thinking about where it could be. It's driving me crazy."

I wrapped my arm around her slender shoulders and gently pulled her toward me. My lips pressed up against her right ear.

"Let me tell you a little story," I whispered.

———

A few years ago I visited Florence. Where I spent most of my days drinking cosmopolitans in a local bar just around the corner from the hotel I was staying in. Hoping for inspiration to strike, to give me an idea for a new book. It didn't happen and I just got drunk.

Anyway, one particular morning, I was joined at my regular table by an elderly gentleman with the most remarkable handlebar moustache. The other significant thing I noticed was the suit he was wearing. Beautifully tailored, all white, except for a bright orange handkerchief neatly folded into a triangle poking out of the top pocket of his jacket.

We exchanged a few meaningless words as strangers often do, discussing the weather and so on, before deciding to share a rather fine bottle of Chianti wine.

By the time the second bottle arrived, the conversation had shifted, and I discovered he was an astrophysicist. More than that, he told me in great detail about his life's work. How he was on a quest to explain the concept of unexpected loss. To be more specific, to solve the mystery of where certain lost items eventually end up and why so many vanish with no logical explanation.

Maurice, that was his name, by the way, had a theory. One he tried to bring to life with a lot of scribbling and the drawing of diagrams on the white tablecloth with a blue Biro. All the time speaking with enthusiasm about the disappearance of lost keys, jewelry, umbrellas, and all manner of everyday objects.

His eureka moment came as our waiter topped up our glasses with a third bottle.

According to him, hiding somewhere between our world and another dimension is a tear in the fabric of time and space. A disruption in the magnetic field that he said surrounded our planet.

He believed that this anomaly was responsible for literally making random objects vanish; as to where they finally ended up, was still a work in process.

I can clearly remember the moment when he banged the table with his fist, startling the other patrons in the bar, his eyes fixed firmly on mine.

"People too!" he shouted. "Why do you think so many missing person cases are never solved?"

I nodded in agreement, anything to get him to calm down and lower his voice.

It was then I noticed the sad expression appear across his wrinkled face as he slumped back into the chair.

He calmly reached inside his jacket and took out a brown leather wallet. Opened it and passed it over to me with a deep sigh.

In the sleeve of the wallet was an old black and white photograph of a young woman standing on a beach. She was smiling.

Maurice took the wallet back.

"Even love can be lost without any logical explanation," he muttered quietly under his breath.

I reached into the bowl of pistachios, my fingers searching through the empty shells, finally finding one that was still intact.

"And? What did he say next?" Lucy demanded, poking me hard in the ribs.

"Oh, nothing, that was it, really. We said our goodbyes and I stumbled back along the cobble streets to my hotel."

Lucy watched me eat the last pistachio, eyes staring blankly.

"You know, that is actually an incredibly sad story," she said, picking up the lone white sock and holding it tightly against her chest.

"The best ones always are."

———

"I read somewhere once that 'lost is a lovely place to find yourself.'"

"I guess that all depends on how you got lost in the first place."

On Any Other Day

On any other day
    I would go quietly
    into the mist,
    and be lost
    within the trees
    of forest green—
    to become invisible,
    unseen.

How simple it would be
    to throw this love away,
    to never look back
    and just leave—
    on any other day.

NEVER FORGET

When a relationship ends, no matter how painful, always
remember it is not the end of love.

WE WANDERED

We wandered—
    across stony ground,
    the pebbles beneath
    our feet like cotton balls,
    the bitterly cold wind—
    a warm blanket
    wrapped around
    naked shoulders,
    the scratches
    from thorns,
    playful fingers
    tickling legs.

For nothing
    can take away
    from love's
    gentle touch.

ROMANCE

Romance seldom happens overnight. Sometimes we have to grow the roses before we can give them.

GOODBYE

When you say *goodbye,* please whisper it. Better still, say nothing and just tiptoe quietly out of my life.

CLARITY

"How can you love me when you don't love yourself?"

Now I understand why you said those words to me.

Why you had to let me go.

Only I had the power to destroy the demons lurking deep inside of me.

To find the strength to drag myself out of the dark abyss.

Back into the light.

Toward the lone candle you left burning in the window.

Guiding me back into your waiting arms.

A RAINY AFTERNOON

How wonderful—
    on a rainy afternoon,
    when the space
    between us closes,
    and I can feel
    your warm breath
    caress my neck,
    your legs wrapped
    around my waist,
    winter's song
    playing softly,
    while we fuck
    beneath the covers,
    in rhythm
    with the raindrops.

A MEMORY CAPTURED

There were moments, fleeting shadows, when the sunlight caught her hair, like a '70s photograph taken with a Hasselblad camera.

A cigarette lit and held by pretty red lips.

A quiet alarm clock and a French bulldog barking.

An untouched croissant sitting on a lilac plate by the side of the bed.

A vase of yesterday's flowers slowly dying on the windowsill.

Her bedroom, our secret darkroom.

Where love slowly came to life in muted colors.

NOBODY'S FOOL

I dreamt of sleep.

My eyelids heavy, the dark circles getting darker by the hour. Sitting upright in my bed, hands holding a silent phone. Waiting for a call, a text, anything to release me from this quiet hell.

Deep down I knew the truth and my wounded heart finally accepted it.

Enough was enough.

I took a deep breath and walked into the bathroom.

Looking in the mirror I could see the courage and defiance slowly returning to a face that had been scarred by sadness these past few weeks.

My lips started to say the words I needed to hear.

"You deserve better than this."

I held my phone up, fingers quickly scrolling through the contacts, and did what I should have done ages ago.

Every trace of you deleted.

Any chance of your return blocked.

The dead weight that had been holding my life back—finally cut loose.

I saw the smile slowly return to my lips in the mirror.

My body overwhelmed by a rush of sheer joy.

I felt like a hot-air balloon.

Soaring upward into a beautiful blue sky.

WAITING FOR LOVE

Love can often be like waiting for a train to arrive and then suddenly realizing you're standing on the wrong platform.

PASSING YEARS

The years will pass,
    sometimes slowly
    other times
    in a blink of an eye,
    but please, my love,
    never fear
    their passing,
    for we will always
    have each other,
    and our love
    will never age.

SMOKE & MIRRORS

She loved to eat strawberry jam on toast.

This gorgeous girl in a white dressing gown, gliding across the black and white checkered kitchen floor like a ballerina on roller skates. Her blond hair tied in a ponytail and just a hint of pale pink lipstick glistening on those sweet lips.

Vivaldi's *Four Seasons* rising up from the speakers of a 1980s Bang & Olufsen stereo that could still spin the dusty vinyl with perfect precision.

I could feel the gentle warmth of the morning sunshine on my unshaven cheek as it streamed in through the windows, sending dancing shadows across my coffee cup. My well-worn copy of *Alice in Wonderland* open on the white marble benchtop.

Justine sat down next to me, picked up my cup, and took a sip.

"Don't you ever get bored of reading that book?" she asked, head peering over my shoulder.

"No, never. I love the absurdity and nonsense. I think of it as a pleasant escape from the dreary headlines in the morning papers. Did you check on the fire? Has it died out yet?"

We had spent the previous night in the little courtyard garden, wrapped in blankets, poking the glowing embers of a fire with sticks, readying the flames for the next article of clothing to be plucked from a green garbage bag. The final remains of James laid to rest.

"It's still smoldering. Well, it was when I last looked earlier. I'll rake the ashes after breakfast and hose it down just to make doubly sure," she said.

"Don't worry about it. I'll take care of it," I replied, taking her hand and gently kissing the back of it.

———

I'd always known Justine as Justine. Even back in the days as uni students when we used to skip our lectures and go surf a curling left-hand break at Rocky Bay. Both of us sporting identical crew cuts, munching down on hotdogs, sitting on the sand, and laughing about our career prospects.

Somehow we managed to scrape enough marks together to graduate. Justine moved away to New York to take a job as an intern in a law firm. I stayed behind to start a design company, my arts degree framed and hung on the wall of my bedroom.

As the years passed, I had gotten married and divorced, sold my design business, and eventually landed a job as an art director for a top New York advertising agency.

At some point during that time, Justine and I also lost touch with each other.

Until one spring afternoon, while I was eating a hotdog in Central Park, a familiar voice jolted me out of my daydream.

"What are you doing here, you loser?"

I spun around and almost fell off the park bench with surprise. Standing behind me was this gorgeous woman, dressed in a chic navy blue pinstriped jacket and matching skirt. Her long blond hair caught by the wind and a black briefcase held in her hand. I knew who it was in an instant and felt a wave of joy sweep over my body.

We hugged and talked nonstop until the sun went down. Catching up on each other's news.

Justine was now a partner at a Midtown law firm and had inherited a brownstone on the Upper West Side from a wealthy aunt. I mentioned I was staying in a hotel while hunting for a new rental apartment. She was having none of that and insisted I stay at her place.

One week turned into a month and the rest as they say is history.

—

"Hello, is anyone at home?" Justine waved her hand in front of my face, snapping me out of my daydream.

I reached for my coffee cup and realized it was empty.

"My bad," Justine giggled. "But you were just staring into space and I couldn't help myself. I'll put another pot on."

"Okay, thanks. I'll go check on the fire while you do that."

One of the nicest things about a Sunday morning was that feeling of inner peace. Knowing you didn't have to rush and do anything in particular.

I unbolted the twin glass doors that led into the courtyard, which was a patch of grass with a border of white rose bushes and a green wrought iron outdoor table with two chairs sitting in the middle.

The blackened charred remains of the fire had made a mess of the lawn. Wisps of gray smoke tainting the fresh scent of autumn air. I uncoiled the hose, turned on the squeaky brass tap, and dampened the area with a burst of water. My mind racing back to Saturday morning.

———

We had found the old battered suitcase while cleaning out the attic. One of the many "must-do" tasks we had put off doing for over a year. It had been filled with junk stored by Justine's deceased aunt, covered in cobwebs and home to a dead rat that we found laying next to a pile of old *Vogue* magazines.

How the suitcase had ended up in the attic was a mystery to Justine. She thought she had thrown it out long ago but her aunt must have hung on to it.

When I opened it, a shocked expression washed over Justine's face, like she had come face-to-face with a ghost. Inside were clothes, *his clothes,* the ones she used to wear when she first arrived in New York and work colleagues knew her as James.

I could see the sadness in Justine's eyes as she picked through the folded trousers, business shirts, ties, socks, and underwear. It was like we had dug up a time capsule filled with all the memories she had wanted to forget.

Transporting her back to that brief period when living a lie seemed preferable to being true to herself. Before she found the courage to finally become the woman she always was.

I put my arms around Justine and held her tight while she sobbed into my shoulder.

I still felt a pang of guilt for not being there for her while she was going through the transformation, the gender realignment therapy and surgery. But like she told me, it was a journey she wanted to do alone and that's why she had decided to cut off all ties to her previous life. Including me.

We emptied the contents of the suitcase into a large garbage bag and decided to light a fire. We spent the night burning all the clothes while swigging whiskey from a bottle and sharing stories about our old uni days.

I remembered the very first time she told me her big secret. It was at a summer beach party and we had been introduced to each other by a friend of mine. Right from the start, we just clicked.

We ended up smoking a joint in the dunes, watching the waves break. Chatting about surfing, gaming, and other stuff. And then mid-conversation the words suddenly spilled out.

"Have you any idea what it feels like to be a woman trapped in the body of a man?"

At first I wasn't sure how to react. I think I made some kind of stupid joke about how it was just my luck to meet a girl at a party who dressed like a dude. We both laughed and from that point onward I accepted James as Justine and our friendship grew.

But the truth was, I had no idea how it felt to be her; how could I?

———

Justine came out to the courtyard holding a cup of freshly brewed coffee.

A lock of blond hair falling down her forehead, the strands glowing in the sunlight.

"Here you go," she said handing me the white china cup. Her eyes suddenly spotting the tears rolling down my cheeks. "Hey, what's wrong?"

She took the cup back from my hands and placed it down on the table.

"I'm so sorry."

I felt her arms wrap around my waist as she pulled me tightly into a warm embrace.

"I'm so sorry, Justine," I repeated. "I never should have let you go. I should have been there for you, stayed with you, protected you."

"Stop. Look at me," she said, cupping my face in the palms of her hands. Her eyes welling up with tears. "You were always there for me and the only thing that matters is that you're here with me now. It was my decision to leave but it was fate that brought us back together. God, I never thought I would ever get to know what happiness feels like. Never believed for a second I would find true love in this cold and callous world. But I did. We did. I love you. I love you more than life itself."

—

Her lips pressed against mine and we kissed like never before. A new fire lit, but this time, deep within our hearts.

Both of us tumbling down a rabbit hole where Wonderland waited.

Far away from a past that no longer haunted us.

To this beautiful place.

Where smoke and mirrors ceased to exist.

Thank You

I wrote this book alone, but we have traveled through its pages together.

And although it is time to part ways, I have a feeling we shall meet again.

Maybe back at the beginning of *Smoke & Mirrors*.

After all, it was written to be read more than once—on glorious sunshine mornings or during those dark stormy nights when sleep seems impossible.

Hopefully our paths will cross in my other books too.

Dirty Pretty Things and *Bitter Sweet Love*.

Until then, please stay in touch and feel free to share your thoughts and photographs on my Facebook, Twitter, and Instagram pages.

I cannot thank you enough for your kind support.

Much appreciated.

I believe in you.

—Michael xo

ACKNOWLEDGMENTS

To my extraordinary literary agent, Al Zuckerman, I cannot thank you enough. You are always there for me when it truly matters and I am in a far better place because of you. Thank you also to Samantha Wekstein and the rest of the team at Writers House, New York.

Thank you so much, Kirsty Melville, Patty Rice, and everyone at Andrews McMeel for your wonderful support and hard work. *Smoke & Mirrors* is our third book together and I'm delighted to have you as a partner and traveling companion on yet another exciting journey.

Tinca Veerman, once again your gorgeous artwork is on the cover of my book. I am so grateful for your generosity and incredible talent. Thank you for being you.

To Oliver, my brilliant son who keeps growing taller with every book I write. I love you more than all the hours, minutes, and seconds you spend playing Overwatch.

SMOKE & MIRRORS

Mum and Dad, thank you for always keeping the front door open for me, a stunning Swan Valley bottle of red on standby, and a delicious spaghetti bolognese bubbling away on the stove top.

To my grandmother, Doris, who is heading toward 100 years old, I think about you all the time.

To Genevieve, my amazing sister, thanks for your unwavering support and laughter. Ryder, keep writing those strange stories and never let a teacher tell you otherwise.

Thank you to all my friends who keep my wine glass constantly topped up.

And another big thank-you to all my lovely readers.

ABOUT THE AUTHOR

Michael Faudet is the author of the international bestsellers *Dirty Pretty Things* and *Bitter Sweet Love*. His whimsical and often erotic writing has captured the hearts and minds of readers from everywhere. Both of his books have been nominated in the Goodreads Choice Awards for Best Poetry. *Dirty Pretty Things* was selected by Sylvia Whitman, the owner of the iconic Shakespeare and Company bookstore in Paris, as one of her favorite books of 2016.

Before turning his hand to writing books, Michael enjoyed a successful career in advertising as an award-winning executive creative director, managing creative departments in cities around the world.

Michael is represented by Writers House, New York.

He currently lives in New Zealand in a little house by the sea with girlfriend and author Lang Leav.

INDEX

Andrews McMeel Publishing
a division of Andrews McMeel Universal
1130 Walnut Street, Kansas City, Missouri 64106

www.andrewsmcmeel.com

www.michaelfaudet.com

18 19 20 21 22 BVG 10 9 8 7 6 5 4 3 2

ISBN: 978-1-4494-8990-8

Library of Congress Control Number: 2017951775

The Fell Types are digitally reproduced by Igino Marini.
www.iginomarini.com

Cover art by Tinca Veerman
www.tincaveerman.com

Editor: Patty Rice
Art Director, Designer: Julie Barnes
Production Editor: David Shaw
Production Manager: Cliff Koehler

ATTENTION: SCHOOLS AND BUSINESSES
Andrews McMeel books are available at quantity discounts with bulk purchase for
educational, business, or sales promotional use. For information, please e-mail the
Andrews McMeel Publishing Special Sales Department: specialsales@amuniversal.com.

Join Michael Faudet on the following:

Facebook

Tumblr

Twitter

Instagram